AF800146

Password Organizer

A Secure Offline Reference for All Your Accounts

Maxwell Stirling

2026

Contents

How to Use This Book

Welcome to your personal password organizer. This book is designed to be a simple, reliable, offline reference for all of your login credentials, account details, and digital security information. No batteries required, no software updates, and no risk of a cloud breach exposing your data.

How This Book Is Organized

The main section of this book is divided alphabetically from **A through Z**. Each letter contains entry blocks where you can record the details for websites and services that start with that letter. For example, your Amazon account would go under **A**, your Netflix account under **N**, and so on.

Each entry block includes fields for:

- **Website** — The name of the service or website
- **URL** — The web address you visit to log in
- **Username** — Your login name or user ID
- **Password** — Your account password
- **Email** — The email address associated with the account
- **Security Question** — The backup question used for account recovery
- **Answer** — Your answer to the security question
- **Notes** — Any additional details (account number, PIN, phone number on file, etc.)

Each letter has space for **12 entries**, spread across 4 pages. If you need more room for a particular letter, use the **Notes** section at the back of the book for overflow entries.

Tips for Getting the Most Out of This Book

Use pencil. Passwords change. Services get cancelled. Writing in pencil means you can erase and update entries without making a mess. A good mechanical pencil with a quality eraser is ideal.

Be consistent. Decide on a system and stick with it. If you file your Google account under **G**, do not also file it under **E** for email. Pick one location and note cross-references if needed.

Keep it secure. This book contains the keys to your digital life. Store it in a locked drawer, a home safe, or another secure location. Do not leave it on your desk, in your car, or anywhere visitors can casually access it.

Update regularly. When you change a password, update this book immediately. A password organizer is only useful if it is current.

Start with what matters most. You do not need to fill in every account on day one. Begin with your most important accounts — email, banking, and social media — and add others as you encounter them.

Additional Sections

Beyond the A–Z password pages, this book includes several bonus sections:

- **Password Security Tips** — Practical guidance on creating strong passwords and staying safe online
- **Wi-Fi Passwords** — A dedicated section for home, work, and frequently visited network credentials
- **Subscription Tracker** — Keep tabs on your monthly and annual subscriptions and their costs
- **Emergency Contacts** — Important phone numbers and account details for emergencies
- **Security Questions & Answers** — A master reference for your security question responses
- **Notes** — Lined pages for anything else you need to record

Turn the page to review the security tips, then begin filling in your accounts. Your future self will thank you.

Password Security Tips

Your passwords are the front door to your digital life. Every email account, bank login, social media profile, and online store you use is protected by a string of characters that either keeps intruders out or invites them in. The difference between a strong password and a weak one can be the difference between a secure account and a devastating breach.

This chapter provides practical, actionable guidance on creating and managing strong passwords. Even if you consider yourself fairly security-savvy, a quick review of these fundamentals is always worthwhile. Threats evolve constantly, and habits that were adequate five years ago may be dangerously outdated today.

Why Strong Passwords Matter

Every year, security researchers publish lists of the most commonly used passwords. Every year, "123456," "password," and "qwerty" appear near the top. Millions of people continue to use these laughably weak credentials, and millions of accounts are compromised as a result.

Here is what is at stake when you use a weak or reused password:

Financial loss. If an attacker gains access to your banking, PayPal, or credit card accounts, they can drain funds, make unauthorized purchases, or open new lines of credit in your name. Recovery can take weeks or months.

Identity theft. Your email account is often the master key to everything else. With access to your email, an attacker can reset passwords on dozens of other services, intercept sensitive communications, and impersonate you to friends, family, and colleagues.

Privacy violations. Personal photos, private messages, medical records, and legal documents stored in cloud services become accessible to anyone who cracks your password.

Reputational damage. Attackers who gain access to social media accounts can post offensive content, send malicious messages to your contacts, or use your identity to run scams.

The core problem is simple: if your password is easy for you to guess, it is easy for an attacker to guess. And modern attackers do not guess one password at a time — they use automated tools that can test billions of combinations per second.

Anatomy of a Strong Password

A strong password has three essential qualities: **length**, **complexity**, and **uniqueness**.

Length

Length is the single most important factor in password strength. Each additional character multiplies the number of possible combinations an attacker must try. A 6-character password using only lowercase letters has about 308 million possible combinations. That sounds like a lot, but a modern computer can crack it in seconds. An 8-character password with mixed case and numbers has roughly 218 billion combinations — better, but still crackable in hours. A 16-character password with mixed case, numbers, and symbols has more combinations than there are atoms in the solar system.

Minimum recommended length: 12 characters. Aim for 16 or more for your most important accounts (email, banking, primary social media).

Complexity

Complexity means using a mix of character types:

- Uppercase letters (A–Z)
- Lowercase letters (a–z)
- Numbers (0–9)
- Symbols (!@#$%^&*+-=?)

A password that uses all four character types is significantly harder to crack than one using only lowercase letters, even at the same length. However, complexity without length is not enough. "P@s5" is complex but trivially short. Prioritize length first, then add complexity.

Uniqueness

Every account should have its own unique password. This is perhaps the most important rule and the one most frequently broken. If you reuse the same password across multiple sites, a breach at one service exposes every account that shares that password. Attackers know that people reuse passwords, and one of the first things they do after obtaining stolen credentials is test them against banking sites, email providers, and social media platforms.

Never reuse a password. Ever. This book makes it easy to maintain unique passwords for every account because you have a dedicated place to record each one.

How to Create Memorable but Strong Passwords

The challenge is clear: you need long, complex, unique passwords for dozens of accounts, and you need to be able to create them reliably. Here are two proven methods.

The Passphrase Method

Instead of a single word, use a phrase of four or more unrelated words. The randomness of the word selection is what provides security.

Examples:

- `correct horse battery staple` (classic example — 28 characters)
- `marble telescope sandwich hurricane` (35 characters)
- `blanket seven railroad penguin` (30 characters)

To add complexity, capitalize one word, substitute a number, and insert a symbol:

- `marble Telescope 4sandwich!hurricane`
- `Blanket7 railroad-penguin`

Passphrases are long, which makes them strong. They are also far easier to remember than a random string like `xK#9mP2$vL`. You can even create a mental image to lock the phrase in memory: picture a penguin riding a railroad while wrapped in a blanket. Absurd images are memorable images.

The Substitution Method

Start with a sentence that is meaningful to you, then extract and transform it:

1. Choose a sentence: "My daughter Sarah was born in Portland in 2005"
2. Take the first letter of each word: `MdSwbiPi2`
3. Add symbols and adjust: `MdSwb!Pi2005#`

This gives you a 13-character password that looks random but is easy for you to reconstruct from the original sentence. Choose sentences that are personally meaningful but not publicly known — do not use song lyrics, famous quotes, or anything that appears on your social media profiles.

The Dice Method

For maximum security, use a method based on true randomness. Roll five dice and look up the corresponding word in a "diceware" word list (freely available online). Repeat four to six times to build a passphrase. Because the words are selected by physical dice rolls rather than human choice, the result is genuinely random and extremely difficult to crack.

What NOT to Use as Passwords

Attackers maintain massive dictionaries of common passwords and predictable patterns. Avoid the following:

- **Your name, your spouse's name, your children's names, or your pet's name.** These are among the first things an attacker will try, especially if they have access to your social media profiles.
- **Birthdates, anniversaries, or phone numbers.** Any date associated with you is low-hanging fruit.
- **"password," "123456," "qwerty," "letmein," or "admin."** These appear in every breached-password database on the planet.
- **Single dictionary words.** Even uncommon words like "chrysanthemum" are trivially cracked by dictionary attacks.
- **Simple keyboard patterns.** "zxcvbn," "asdfgh," and "1qaz2wsx" are all well-known patterns that attackers test early.
- **Sequences and repetitions.** "abcdef," "111111," and "aabbcc" offer essentially zero security.
- **Passwords you have used before.** If an old password was part of a breach, it is permanently compromised. Never recycle it.
- **Anything that can be found on your social media.** Your hometown, your college, your favorite sports team, your dog's name — all of this is public information and all of it is useless as a password.

Two-Factor Authentication (2FA)

Two-factor authentication adds a second layer of security beyond your password. Even if an attacker obtains your password, they cannot access your account without the second factor.

How 2FA Works

When you log in with 2FA enabled, you enter your password as usual (the first factor — something you know). You are then prompted for a second factor — something you have. This is typically one of the following:

- **A code sent via text message (SMS).** A 6-digit code is texted to your phone. This is the most common form of 2FA but also the least secure, because text messages can be intercepted through SIM-swapping attacks.
- **An authenticator app code.** Apps like Google Authenticator, Microsoft Authenticator, or Authy generate time-based codes that change every 30 seconds. This is more secure than SMS because the codes are generated on your device and never transmitted over a network.
- **A hardware security key.** Physical devices like YubiKey plug into your computer or tap against your phone to verify your identity. This is the most secure form of 2FA because the key must be physically present.
- **Biometric verification.** Fingerprint or face recognition on your device. Increasingly common and very convenient.

Where to Enable 2FA

At a minimum, enable two-factor authentication on:

- Your primary email account (this is the most critical — your email is the recovery path for almost everything else)
- Your bank and financial accounts
- Social media accounts
- Cloud storage services (Google Drive, Dropbox, iCloud)
- Any account that stores payment information

Most major services now support 2FA. Look in the account settings under "Security" or "Login Options." The few minutes it takes to set up can prevent catastrophic breaches.

Recording Your 2FA Backup Codes

When you enable 2FA, most services provide a set of one-time backup codes. These are your lifeline if you lose access to your phone or authenticator app. **Record these backup codes in the Notes field of the corresponding entry in this book.** Treat them with the same care as your passwords.

What to Do If You Think You Have Been Hacked

If you notice suspicious activity on any of your accounts — unfamiliar login alerts, password reset emails you did not request, transactions you did not make, or messages sent from your account that you did not write — act immediately. Speed matters.

Step 1: Change the password on the affected account. Do this from a device you trust (not a public computer). Create a new, strong, unique password and record it in this book.

Step 2: Change the password on your primary email account. If the attacker accessed your email, they may have already initiated password resets on other services. Secure your email first.

Step 3: Enable or verify 2FA. If 2FA was not enabled on the compromised account, enable it now. If it was enabled and the attacker still got in, check whether your 2FA method was compromised (especially if you were using SMS-based codes).

Step 4: Check for unauthorized changes. Look for forwarding rules in your email, connected apps you did not authorize, recovery email addresses or phone numbers that are not yours, and shipping addresses added to shopping accounts.

Step 5: Review other accounts that share the same password. If you reused the compromised password anywhere, change it on every account immediately. This is exactly the scenario that unique passwords prevent.

Step 6: Check your financial accounts. Review recent transactions on all bank accounts and credit cards. Report any unauthorized activity to your financial institution immediately.

Step 7: Run a security scan. Use reputable antivirus software to scan your computer and phone for malware that may have captured your credentials.

Step 8: Consider a credit freeze. If sensitive personal information was exposed, contact the major credit bureaus to place a freeze on your credit file, preventing anyone from opening new accounts in your name.

Step 9: Document everything. Record what happened, when you discovered it, and what steps you took. This documentation is valuable if you need to file a fraud report, dispute charges, or work with law enforcement.

Password Manager Software

This book is a reliable offline backup, but digital password managers offer complementary benefits. A password manager is an application that stores all of your passwords in an encrypted vault, protected by a single master password. Many can also generate strong random passwords for you and automatically fill in login forms.

Popular and reputable password managers include:

- **Bitwarden** — Open source, free tier available, works across all platforms
- **1Password** — User-friendly, excellent family and team sharing features
- **KeePass** — Free, open source, stores your vault locally (no cloud required)
- **Dashlane** — Polished interface, includes VPN and dark web monitoring features

Using both a digital password manager and this physical book gives you the best of both worlds: the convenience and autofill capability of software, plus a secure offline backup that works even when your devices fail, your subscription lapses, or you simply cannot remember your master password.

Important: If you use a password manager, your master password is the single most important password you have. Make it exceptionally strong (20+ characters), never use it anywhere else, and record it in this book.

Common Scams and Phishing Attacks

Even the strongest password is useless if you hand it directly to an attacker. Phishing attacks are designed to trick you into doing exactly that.

Email Phishing

You receive an email that appears to be from your bank, a shipping company, or a service you use. It warns of suspicious activity, a failed payment, or an account suspension. It includes a link to "verify your account" or "update your payment information." The link leads to a fake website that looks identical to the real one. When you enter your login credentials, the attacker captures them.

How to spot it: Check the sender's actual email address (not just the display name). Hover over links before clicking to see the real URL. Legitimate companies will never ask you to verify your password via email. When in doubt, go directly to the website by typing the URL in your browser rather than clicking any link in the email.

SMS and Phone Phishing (Smishing and Vishing)

Similar to email phishing, but delivered via text message or phone call. You might receive a text claiming to be from your bank with a link, or a phone call from someone claiming to be tech support who needs your login credentials to "fix a problem."

How to spot it: Your bank will never ask for your full password over the phone. Tech support will never cold-call you. If you receive a suspicious call, hang up and call the company directly using the number on their official website or the back of your card.

Fake Login Pages

Attackers create convincing replicas of popular login pages and distribute links through email, social media, or even search engine ads. The URL will be slightly different from the legitimate site — perhaps "arnazon.com" instead of "amazon.com" or "paypa1.com" instead of "paypal.com."

How to spot it: Always check the URL in your browser's address bar before entering credentials. Look for the correct domain spelling and a padlock icon indicating a secure connection. Bookmark your most important sites and use those bookmarks to navigate rather than clicking links.

The Bottom Line

No single security measure is perfect. Strong, unique passwords are your foundation. Two-factor authentication is your reinforcement. Vigilance against phishing is your daily practice. Together, they form a defense that will protect you against the vast majority of threats.

This book is one piece of that defense. Use it consistently, keep it secure, and keep it up to date. Your digital security is worth the effort.

Password Pages

A

A

Website:

URL:

Username:

Password:

Email:

Security Question:

Answer:

Notes:

Website:

URL:

Username:

Password:

Email:

Security Question:

Answer:

Notes:

Website:

URL:

Username:

Password:

Email:

Security Question: ______________________________

Answer: ______________________________

Notes: ______________________________

A

Website:
URL:
Username:
Password:
Email:
Security Question:
Answer:
Notes:

Website:
URL:
Username:
Password:
Email:
Security Question:
Answer:
Notes:

Website:
URL:
Username:
Password:
Email:

Security Question: ______________________________

Answer: ______________________________

Notes: ______________________________

A

Website:

URL:

Username:

Password:

Email:

Security Question:

Answer:

Notes:

Website:

URL:

Username:

Password:

Email:

Security Question:

Answer:

Notes:

Website:

URL:

Username:

Password:

Email:

Security Question: ______________________________

Answer: ______________________________

Notes: ______________________________

A

Website:

URL:

Username:

Password:

Email:

Security Question:

Answer:

Notes:

Website:

URL:

Username:

Password:

Email:

Security Question:

Answer:

Notes:

Website:

URL:

Username:

Password:

Email:

Security Question: ______________________________

Answer: ______________________________

Notes: ______________________________

B

B

Website:
URL:
Username:
Password:
Email:
Security Question:
Answer:
Notes:

Website:
URL:
Username:
Password:
Email:
Security Question:
Answer:
Notes:

Website:
URL:
Username:
Password:
Email:

Security Question: ______________________________

Answer: ______________________________

Notes: ______________________________

B

Website:
URL:
Username:
Password:
Email:
Security Question:
Answer:
Notes:

Website:
URL:
Username:
Password:
Email:
Security Question:
Answer:
Notes:

Website:
URL:
Username:
Password:
Email:

Security Question: ___________________________

Answer: ___________________________

Notes: ___________________________

B

Website: ______

URL: ______

Username: ______

Password: ______

Email: ______

Security Question: ______

Answer: ______

Notes: ______

Website: ______

URL: ______

Username: ______

Password: ______

Email: ______

Security Question: ______

Answer: ______

Notes: ______

Website: ______

URL: ______

Username: ______

Password: ______

Email: ______

Security Question: ______________________________

Answer: ______________________________

Notes: ______________________________

B

Website:
URL:
Username:
Password:
Email:
Security Question:
Answer:
Notes:

Website:
URL:
Username:
Password:
Email:
Security Question:
Answer:
Notes:

Website:
URL:
Username:
Password:
Email:

Security Question: ______________________________

Answer: ______________________________

Notes: ______________________________

C

C

Website:

URL:

Username:

Password:

Email:

Security Question:

Answer:

Notes:

Website:

URL:

Username:

Password:

Email:

Security Question:

Answer:

Notes:

Website:

URL:

Username:

Password:

Email:

Security Question: ______________________________

Answer: ______________________________

Notes: ______________________________

C

Website:

URL:

Username:

Password:

Email:

Security Question:

Answer:

Notes:

Website:

URL:

Username:

Password:

Email:

Security Question:

Answer:

Notes:

Website:

URL:

Username:

Password:

Email:

Security Question: ____________________

Answer: ____________________

Notes: ____________________

C

Website:

URL:

Username:

Password:

Email:

Security Question:

Answer:

Notes:

Website:

URL:

Username:

Password:

Email:

Security Question:

Answer:

Notes:

Website:

URL:

Username:

Password:

Email:

Security Question: ______________________________

Answer: ______________________________

Notes: ______________________________

C

Website:
URL:
Username:
Password:
Email:
Security Question:
Answer:
Notes:

Website:
URL:
Username:
Password:
Email:
Security Question:
Answer:
Notes:

Website:
URL:
Username:
Password:
Email:

Security Question: ____

Answer: ____

Notes: ____

D

D

Website:
URL:
Username:
Password:
Email:
Security Question:
Answer:
Notes:

Website:
URL:
Username:
Password:
Email:
Security Question:
Answer:
Notes:

Website:
URL:
Username:
Password:
Email:

Security Question: ______________________________

Answer: ______________________________

Notes: ______________________________

D

Website:
URL:
Username:
Password:
Email:
Security Question:
Answer:
Notes:

Website:
URL:
Username:
Password:
Email:
Security Question:
Answer:
Notes:

Website:
URL:
Username:
Password:
Email:

Security Question: ______________________________

Answer: ______________________________

Notes: ______________________________

D

Website: ____________________

URL: ____________________

Username: ____________________

Password: ____________________

Email: ____________________

Security Question: ____________________

Answer: ____________________

Notes: ____________________

Website: ____________________

URL: ____________________

Username: ____________________

Password: ____________________

Email: ____________________

Security Question: ____________________

Answer: ____________________

Notes: ____________________

Website: ____________________

URL: ____________________

Username: ____________________

Password: ____________________

Email: ____________________

Security Question: ______________________________

Answer: ______________________________

Notes: ______________________________

D

Website:

URL:

Username:

Password:

Email:

Security Question:

Answer:

Notes:

Website:

URL:

Username:

Password:

Email:

Security Question:

Answer:

Notes:

Website:

URL:

Username:

Password:

Email:

Security Question: ___________________________________

Answer: ___________________________________

Notes: ___________________________________

E

E

Website: ______________________

URL: ______________________

Username: ______________________

Password: ______________________

Email: ______________________

Security Question: ______________________

Answer: ______________________

Notes: ______________________

Website: ______________________

URL: ______________________

Username: ______________________

Password: ______________________

Email: ______________________

Security Question: ______________________

Answer: ______________________

Notes: ______________________

Website: ______________________

URL: ______________________

Username: ______________________

Password: ______________________

Email: ______________________

Security Question: ______________________________

Answer: ______________________________

Notes: ______________________________

E

Website:

URL:

Username:

Password:

Email:

Security Question:

Answer:

Notes:

Website:

URL:

Username:

Password:

Email:

Security Question:

Answer:

Notes:

Website:

URL:

Username:

Password:

Email:

Security Question: ______________________________

Answer: ______________________________

Notes: ______________________________

E

Website:

URL:

Username:

Password:

Email:

Security Question:

Answer:

Notes:

Website:

URL:

Username:

Password:

Email:

Security Question:

Answer:

Notes:

Website:

URL:

Username:

Password:

Email:

Security Question: ____________________

Answer: ____________________

Notes: ____________________

E

Website:

URL:

Username:

Password:

Email:

Security Question:

Answer:

Notes:

Website:

URL:

Username:

Password:

Email:

Security Question:

Answer:

Notes:

Website:

URL:

Username:

Password:

Email:

Security Question: ______________________________

Answer: ______________________________

Notes: ______________________________

F

Website:

URL:

Username:

Password:

Email:

Security Question:

Answer:

Notes:

Website:

URL:

Username:

Password:

Email:

Security Question:

Answer:

Notes:

Website:

URL:

Username:

Password:

Email:

Security Question: ______________________________

Answer: ______________________________

Notes: ______________________________

F

Website:

URL:

Username:

Password:

Email:

Security Question:

Answer:

Notes:

Website:

URL:

Username:

Password:

Email:

Security Question:

Answer:

Notes:

Website:

URL:

Username:

Password:

Email:

Security Question: ____________________

Answer: ____________________

Notes: ____________________

F

Website:

URL:

Username:

Password:

Email:

Security Question:

Answer:

Notes:

Website:

URL:

Username:

Password:

Email:

Security Question:

Answer:

Notes:

Website:

URL:

Username:

Password:

Email:

Security Question: ______________________________

Answer: ______________________________

Notes: ______________________________

F

Website:
URL:
Username:
Password:
Email:
Security Question:
Answer:
Notes:

Website:
URL:
Username:
Password:
Email:
Security Question:
Answer:
Notes:

Website:
URL:
Username:
Password:
Email:

Security Question: ____

Answer: ____

Notes: ____

G

G

Website:
URL:
Username:
Password:
Email:
Security Question:
Answer:
Notes:

Website:
URL:
Username:
Password:
Email:
Security Question:
Answer:
Notes:

Website:
URL:
Username:
Password:
Email:

Security Question: ______________________________

Answer: ______________________________

Notes: ______________________________

G

Website: ____________________

URL: ____________________

Username: ____________________

Password: ____________________

Email: ____________________

Security Question: ____________________

Answer: ____________________

Notes: ____________________

Website: ____________________

URL: ____________________

Username: ____________________

Password: ____________________

Email: ____________________

Security Question: ____________________

Answer: ____________________

Notes: ____________________

Website: ____________________

URL: ____________________

Username: ____________________

Password: ____________________

Email: ____________________

Security Question: ______________________________

Answer: ______________________________

Notes: ______________________________

G

Website:

URL:

Username:

Password:

Email:

Security Question:

Answer:

Notes:

Website:

URL:

Username:

Password:

Email:

Security Question:

Answer:

Notes:

Website:

URL:

Username:

Password:

Email:

Security Question: ______________________________

Answer: ______________________________

Notes: ______________________________

G

Website:
URL:
Username:
Password:
Email:
Security Question:
Answer:
Notes:

Website:
URL:
Username:
Password:
Email:
Security Question:
Answer:
Notes:

Website:
URL:
Username:
Password:
Email:

Security Question: ______________________________

Answer: ______________________________

Notes: ______________________________

H

H

Website:

URL:

Username:

Password:

Email:

Security Question:

Answer:

Notes:

Website:

URL:

Username:

Password:

Email:

Security Question:

Answer:

Notes:

Website:

URL:

Username:

Password:

Email:

Security Question: ______________________________

Answer: ______________________________

Notes: ______________________________

H

Website:
URL:
Username:
Password:
Email:
Security Question:
Answer:
Notes:

Website:
URL:
Username:
Password:
Email:
Security Question:
Answer:
Notes:

Website:
URL:
Username:
Password:
Email:

Security Question: ______________________________

Answer: ______________________________

Notes: ______________________________

H

Website:

URL:

Username:

Password:

Email:

Security Question:

Answer:

Notes:

Website:

URL:

Username:

Password:

Email:

Security Question:

Answer:

Notes:

Website:

URL:

Username:

Password:

Email:

Security Question: ______________________________

Answer: ______________________________

Notes: ______________________________

H

Website:
URL:
Username:
Password:
Email:
Security Question:
Answer:
Notes:

Website:
URL:
Username:
Password:
Email:
Security Question:
Answer:
Notes:

Website:
URL:
Username:
Password:
Email:

Security Question: ______________________________

Answer: ______________________________

Notes: ______________________________

I

I

Website:
URL:
Username:
Password:
Email:
Security Question:
Answer:
Notes:

Website:
URL:
Username:
Password:
Email:
Security Question:
Answer:
Notes:

Website:
URL:
Username:
Password:
Email:

Security Question: ______________________________

Answer: ______________________________

Notes: ______________________________

I

Website: ________________

URL: ________________

Username: ________________

Password: ________________

Email: ________________

Security Question: ________________

Answer: ________________

Notes: ________________

Website: ________________

URL: ________________

Username: ________________

Password: ________________

Email: ________________

Security Question: ________________

Answer: ________________

Notes: ________________

Website: ________________

URL: ________________

Username: ________________

Password: ________________

Email: ________________

Security Question: ______________________________

Answer: ______________________________

Notes: ______________________________

I

Website:
URL:
Username:
Password:
Email:
Security Question:
Answer:
Notes:

Website:
URL:
Username:
Password:
Email:
Security Question:
Answer:
Notes:

Website:
URL:
Username:
Password:
Email:

Security Question: ______________________________

Answer: ______________________________

Notes: ______________________________

I

Website:

URL:

Username:

Password:

Email:

Security Question:

Answer:

Notes:

Website:

URL:

Username:

Password:

Email:

Security Question:

Answer:

Notes:

Website:

URL:

Username:

Password:

Email:

Security Question: ______________________________

Answer: ______________________________

Notes: ______________________________

J

J

Website:

URL:

Username:

Password:

Email:

Security Question:

Answer:

Notes:

Website:

URL:

Username:

Password:

Email:

Security Question:

Answer:

Notes:

Website:

URL:

Username:

Password:

Email:

Security Question: ______________________________

Answer: ______________________________

Notes: ______________________________

J

Website: ______

URL: ______

Username: ______

Password: ______

Email: ______

Security Question: ______

Answer: ______

Notes: ______

Website: ______

URL: ______

Username: ______

Password: ______

Email: ______

Security Question: ______

Answer: ______

Notes: ______

Website: ______

URL: ______

Username: ______

Password: ______

Email: ______

Security Question: ______________________________

Answer: ______________________________

Notes: ______________________________

J

Website:
URL:
Username:
Password:
Email:
Security Question:
Answer:
Notes:

Website:
URL:
Username:
Password:
Email:
Security Question:
Answer:
Notes:

Website:
URL:
Username:
Password:
Email:

Security Question: ______________________________

Answer: ______________________________

Notes: ______________________________

J

Website:

URL:

Username:

Password:

Email:

Security Question:

Answer:

Notes:

Website:

URL:

Username:

Password:

Email:

Security Question:

Answer:

Notes:

Website:

URL:

Username:

Password:

Email:

Security Question: ______________________________

Answer: ______________________________

Notes: ______________________________

K

K

Website:
URL:
Username:
Password:
Email:
Security Question:
Answer:
Notes:

Website:
URL:
Username:
Password:
Email:
Security Question:
Answer:
Notes:

Website:
URL:
Username:
Password:
Email:

Security Question: ______________________________

Answer: ______________________________

Notes: ______________________________

K

Website:

URL:

Username:

Password:

Email:

Security Question:

Answer:

Notes:

Website:

URL:

Username:

Password:

Email:

Security Question:

Answer:

Notes:

Website:

URL:

Username:

Password:

Email:

Security Question: ______________________________________

Answer: ______________________________________

Notes: ______________________________________

K

Website:

URL:

Username:

Password:

Email:

Security Question:

Answer:

Notes:

Website:

URL:

Username:

Password:

Email:

Security Question:

Answer:

Notes:

Website:

URL:

Username:

Password:

Email:

Security Question: ______________________________

Answer: ______________________________

Notes: ______________________________

K

Website:

URL:

Username:

Password:

Email:

Security Question:

Answer:

Notes:

Website:

URL:

Username:

Password:

Email:

Security Question:

Answer:

Notes:

Website:

URL:

Username:

Password:

Email:

Security Question: ______________________________

Answer: ______________________________

Notes: ______________________________

L

L

Website:
URL:
Username:
Password:
Email:
Security Question:
Answer:
Notes:

Website:
URL:
Username:
Password:
Email:
Security Question:
Answer:
Notes:

Website:
URL:
Username:
Password:
Email:

Security Question: ______________________________

Answer: ______________________________

Notes: ______________________________

L

Website: ____________________

URL: ____________________

Username: ____________________

Password: ____________________

Email: ____________________

Security Question: ____________________

Answer: ____________________

Notes: ____________________

Website: ____________________

URL: ____________________

Username: ____________________

Password: ____________________

Email: ____________________

Security Question: ____________________

Answer: ____________________

Notes: ____________________

Website: ____________________

URL: ____________________

Username: ____________________

Password: ____________________

Email: ____________________

Security Question: ______________________________

Answer: ______________________________

Notes: ______________________________

L

Website:
URL:
Username:
Password:
Email:
Security Question:
Answer:
Notes:

Website:
URL:
Username:
Password:
Email:
Security Question:
Answer:
Notes:

Website:
URL:
Username:
Password:
Email:

Security Question: ______________________________

Answer: ______________________________

Notes: ______________________________

L

Website:
URL:
Username:
Password:
Email:
Security Question:
Answer:
Notes:

Website:
URL:
Username:
Password:
Email:
Security Question:
Answer:
Notes:

Website:
URL:
Username:
Password:
Email:

Security Question: ________________________________

Answer: ________________________________

Notes: ________________________________

M

M

Website:
URL:
Username:
Password:
Email:
Security Question:
Answer:
Notes:

Website:
URL:
Username:
Password:
Email:
Security Question:
Answer:
Notes:

Website:
URL:
Username:
Password:
Email:

Security Question: ______________________________

Answer: ______________________________

Notes: ______________________________

M

Website:

URL:

Username:

Password:

Email:

Security Question:

Answer:

Notes:

Website:

URL:

Username:

Password:

Email:

Security Question:

Answer:

Notes:

Website:

URL:

Username:

Password:

Email:

Security Question: ___________________________________

Answer: ___________________________________

Notes: ___________________________________

M

Website:
URL:
Username:
Password:
Email:
Security Question:
Answer:
Notes:

Website:
URL:
Username:
Password:
Email:
Security Question:
Answer:
Notes:

Website:
URL:
Username:
Password:
Email:

Security Question: ______________________________

Answer: ______________________________

Notes: ______________________________

M

Website:

URL:

Username:

Password:

Email:

Security Question:

Answer:

Notes:

Website:

URL:

Username:

Password:

Email:

Security Question:

Answer:

Notes:

Website:

URL:

Username:

Password:

Email:

Security Question: ______________________________

Answer: ______________________________

Notes: ______________________________

N

N

Website:

URL:

Username:

Password:

Email:

Security Question:

Answer:

Notes:

Website:

URL:

Username:

Password:

Email:

Security Question:

Answer:

Notes:

Website:

URL:

Username:

Password:

Email:

Security Question: ______________________________

Answer: ______________________________

Notes: ______________________________

N

Website:
URL:
Username:
Password:
Email:
Security Question:
Answer:
Notes:

Website:
URL:
Username:
Password:
Email:
Security Question:
Answer:
Notes:

Website:
URL:
Username:
Password:
Email:

Security Question: ______________________________

Answer: ______________________________

Notes: ______________________________

N

Website:

URL:

Username:

Password:

Email:

Security Question:

Answer:

Notes:

Website:

URL:

Username:

Password:

Email:

Security Question:

Answer:

Notes:

Website:

URL:

Username:

Password:

Email:

Security Question: ________________________________

Answer: ________________________________

Notes: ________________________________

N

Website:
URL:
Username:
Password:
Email:
Security Question:
Answer:
Notes:

Website:
URL:
Username:
Password:
Email:
Security Question:
Answer:
Notes:

Website:
URL:
Username:
Password:
Email:

Security Question: ______________________________

Answer: ______________________________

Notes: ______________________________

O

O

Website:

URL:

Username:

Password:

Email:

Security Question:

Answer:

Notes:

Website:

URL:

Username:

Password:

Email:

Security Question:

Answer:

Notes:

Website:

URL:

Username:

Password:

Email:

Security Question: ______________________________

Answer: ______________________________

Notes: ______________________________

O

Website:
URL:
Username:
Password:
Email:
Security Question:
Answer:
Notes:

Website:
URL:
Username:
Password:
Email:
Security Question:
Answer:
Notes:

Website:
URL:
Username:
Password:
Email:

Security Question: ______________________________

Answer: ______________________________

Notes: ______________________________

O

Website:

URL:

Username:

Password:

Email:

Security Question:

Answer:

Notes:

Website:

URL:

Username:

Password:

Email:

Security Question:

Answer:

Notes:

Website:

URL:

Username:

Password:

Email:

Security Question: ______________________________

Answer: ______________________________

Notes: ______________________________

Website:

URL:

Username:

Password:

Email:

Security Question:

Answer:

Notes:

Website:

URL:

Username:

Password:

Email:

Security Question:

Answer:

Notes:

Website:

URL:

Username:

Password:

Email:

Security Question: ___________________________________

Answer: ___________________________________

Notes: ___________________________________

P

P

Website:

URL:

Username:

Password:

Email:

Security Question:

Answer:

Notes:

Website:

URL:

Username:

Password:

Email:

Security Question:

Answer:

Notes:

Website:

URL:

Username:

Password:

Email:

Security Question: ______________________________

Answer: ______________________________

Notes: ______________________________

P

Website:

URL:

Username:

Password:

Email:

Security Question:

Answer:

Notes:

Website:

URL:

Username:

Password:

Email:

Security Question:

Answer:

Notes:

Website:

URL:

Username:

Password:

Email:

Security Question: ______________________________

Answer: ______________________________

Notes: ______________________________

P

Website:

URL:

Username:

Password:

Email:

Security Question:

Answer:

Notes:

Website:

URL:

Username:

Password:

Email:

Security Question:

Answer:

Notes:

Website:

URL:

Username:

Password:

Email:

Security Question: ______________________________

Answer: ______________________________

Notes: ______________________________

P

Website:
URL:
Username:
Password:
Email:
Security Question:
Answer:
Notes:

Website:
URL:
Username:
Password:
Email:
Security Question:
Answer:
Notes:

Website:
URL:
Username:
Password:
Email:

Security Question: ______________________________

Answer: ______________________________

Notes: ______________________________

Q

Q

Website:
URL:
Username:
Password:
Email:
Security Question:
Answer:
Notes:

Website:
URL:
Username:
Password:
Email:
Security Question:
Answer:
Notes:

Website:
URL:
Username:
Password:
Email:

Security Question: ______________________________

Answer: ______________________________

Notes: ______________________________

Q

Website:
URL:
Username:
Password:
Email:
Security Question:
Answer:
Notes:

Website:
URL:
Username:
Password:
Email:
Security Question:
Answer:
Notes:

Website:
URL:
Username:
Password:
Email:

Security Question: ______________________________

Answer: ______________________________

Notes: ______________________________

Q

Website:

URL:

Username:

Password:

Email:

Security Question:

Answer:

Notes:

Website:

URL:

Username:

Password:

Email:

Security Question:

Answer:

Notes:

Website:

URL:

Username:

Password:

Email:

Security Question: ______________________________

Answer: ______________________________

Notes: ______________________________

Q

Website:

URL:

Username:

Password:

Email:

Security Question:

Answer:

Notes:

Website:

URL:

Username:

Password:

Email:

Security Question:

Answer:

Notes:

Website:

URL:

Username:

Password:

Email:

Security Question: ______________________________

Answer: ______________________________

Notes: ______________________________

R

R

Website:
URL:
Username:
Password:
Email:
Security Question:
Answer:
Notes:

Website:
URL:
Username:
Password:
Email:
Security Question:
Answer:
Notes:

Website:
URL:
Username:
Password:
Email:

Security Question: ______________________________

Answer: ______________________________

Notes: ______________________________

R

Website: ______

URL: ______

Username: ______

Password: ______

Email: ______

Security Question: ______

Answer: ______

Notes: ______

Website: ______

URL: ______

Username: ______

Password: ______

Email: ______

Security Question: ______

Answer: ______

Notes: ______

Website: ______

URL: ______

Username: ______

Password: ______

Email: ______

Security Question: ____________________

Answer: ____________________

Notes: ____________________

R

Website:
URL:
Username:
Password:
Email:
Security Question:
Answer:
Notes:

Website:
URL:
Username:
Password:
Email:
Security Question:
Answer:
Notes:

Website:
URL:
Username:
Password:
Email:

Security Question: ___

Answer: ___

Notes: ___

R

Website: ____________________
URL: ____________________
Username: ____________________
Password: ____________________
Email: ____________________
Security Question: ____________________
Answer: ____________________
Notes: ____________________

Website: ____________________
URL: ____________________
Username: ____________________
Password: ____________________
Email: ____________________
Security Question: ____________________
Answer: ____________________
Notes: ____________________

Website: ____________________
URL: ____________________
Username: ____________________
Password: ____________________
Email: ____________________

Security Question: ______________________________

Answer: ______________________________

Notes: ______________________________

S

S

Website: ______

URL: ______

Username: ______

Password: ______

Email: ______

Security Question: ______

Answer: ______

Notes: ______

Website: ______

URL: ______

Username: ______

Password: ______

Email: ______

Security Question: ______

Answer: ______

Notes: ______

Website: ______

URL: ______

Username: ______

Password: ______

Email: ______

Security Question: ______________________________

Answer: ______________________________

Notes: ______________________________

S

Website:

URL:

Username:

Password:

Email:

Security Question:

Answer:

Notes:

Website:

URL:

Username:

Password:

Email:

Security Question:

Answer:

Notes:

Website:

URL:

Username:

Password:

Email:

Security Question: ______________________________

Answer: ______________________________

Notes: ______________________________

S

Website: ______

URL: ______

Username: ______

Password: ______

Email: ______

Security Question: ______

Answer: ______

Notes: ______

Website: ______

URL: ______

Username: ______

Password: ______

Email: ______

Security Question: ______

Answer: ______

Notes: ______

Website: ______

URL: ______

Username: ______

Password: ______

Email: ______

Security Question: ______________________________

Answer: ______________________________

Notes: ______________________________

S

Website:
URL:
Username:
Password:
Email:
Security Question:
Answer:
Notes:

Website:
URL:
Username:
Password:
Email:
Security Question:
Answer:
Notes:

Website:
URL:
Username:
Password:
Email:

Security Question: ______________________________

Answer: ______________________________

Notes: ______________________________

T

T

Website:

URL:

Username:

Password:

Email:

Security Question:

Answer:

Notes:

Website:

URL:

Username:

Password:

Email:

Security Question:

Answer:

Notes:

Website:

URL:

Username:

Password:

Email:

Security Question: ______________________________

Answer: ______________________________

Notes: ______________________________

T

Website:
URL:
Username:
Password:
Email:
Security Question:
Answer:
Notes:

Website:
URL:
Username:
Password:
Email:
Security Question:
Answer:
Notes:

Website:
URL:
Username:
Password:
Email:

Security Question: ______________________________

Answer: ______________________________

Notes: ______________________________

T

Website:
URL:
Username:
Password:
Email:
Security Question:
Answer:
Notes:

Website:
URL:
Username:
Password:
Email:
Security Question:
Answer:
Notes:

Website:
URL:
Username:
Password:
Email:

Security Question: ______________________________

Answer: ______________________________

Notes: ______________________________

T

Website:
URL:
Username:
Password:
Email:
Security Question:
Answer:
Notes:

Website:
URL:
Username:
Password:
Email:
Security Question:
Answer:
Notes:

Website:
URL:
Username:
Password:
Email:

Security Question: ______________________________

Answer: ______________________________

Notes: ______________________________

U

U

Website:
URL:
Username:
Password:
Email:
Security Question:
Answer:
Notes:

Website:
URL:
Username:
Password:
Email:
Security Question:
Answer:
Notes:

Website:
URL:
Username:
Password:
Email:

Security Question: ______________________________

Answer: ______________________________

Notes: ______________________________

U

Website:
URL:
Username:
Password:
Email:
Security Question:
Answer:
Notes:

Website:
URL:
Username:
Password:
Email:
Security Question:
Answer:
Notes:

Website:
URL:
Username:
Password:
Email:

Security Question: ______________________________

Answer: ______________________________

Notes: ______________________________

U

Website:

URL:

Username:

Password:

Email:

Security Question:

Answer:

Notes:

Website:

URL:

Username:

Password:

Email:

Security Question:

Answer:

Notes:

Website:

URL:

Username:

Password:

Email:

Security Question: ______________________________

Answer: ______________________________

Notes: ______________________________

U

Website:
URL:
Username:
Password:
Email:
Security Question:
Answer:
Notes:

Website:
URL:
Username:
Password:
Email:
Security Question:
Answer:
Notes:

Website:
URL:
Username:
Password:
Email:

Security Question: ____________________

Answer: ____________________

Notes: ____________________

V

V

Website:

URL:

Username:

Password:

Email:

Security Question:

Answer:

Notes:

Website:

URL:

Username:

Password:

Email:

Security Question:

Answer:

Notes:

Website:

URL:

Username:

Password:

Email:

Security Question: ______________________________

Answer: ______________________________

Notes: ______________________________

V

Website:
URL:
Username:
Password:
Email:
Security Question:
Answer:
Notes:

Website:
URL:
Username:
Password:
Email:
Security Question:
Answer:
Notes:

Website:
URL:
Username:
Password:
Email:

Security Question: ______________________________

Answer: ______________________________

Notes: ______________________________

V

Website: ____________________

URL: ____________________

Username: ____________________

Password: ____________________

Email: ____________________

Security Question: ____________________

Answer: ____________________

Notes: ____________________

Website: ____________________

URL: ____________________

Username: ____________________

Password: ____________________

Email: ____________________

Security Question: ____________________

Answer: ____________________

Notes: ____________________

Website: ____________________

URL: ____________________

Username: ____________________

Password: ____________________

Email: ____________________

Security Question: ________________________________

Answer: ________________________________

Notes: ________________________________

V

Website:
URL:
Username:
Password:
Email:
Security Question:
Answer:
Notes:

Website:
URL:
Username:
Password:
Email:
Security Question:
Answer:
Notes:

Website:
URL:
Username:
Password:
Email:

Security Question: ______________________________

Answer: ______________________________

Notes: ______________________________

W

Website: ____________
URL: ____________
Username: ____________
Password: ____________
Email: ____________
Security Question: ____________
Answer: ____________
Notes: ____________

Website: ____________
URL: ____________
Username: ____________
Password: ____________
Email: ____________
Security Question: ____________
Answer: ____________
Notes: ____________

Website: ____________
URL: ____________
Username: ____________
Password: ____________
Email: ____________

Security Question: ______________________________

Answer: ______________________________

Notes: ______________________________

W

Website:

URL:

Username:

Password:

Email:

Security Question:

Answer:

Notes:

Website:

URL:

Username:

Password:

Email:

Security Question:

Answer:

Notes:

Website:

URL:

Username:

Password:

Email:

Security Question: ______________________________

Answer: ______________________________

Notes: ______________________________

W

Website:
URL:
Username:
Password:
Email:
Security Question:
Answer:
Notes:

Website:
URL:
Username:
Password:
Email:
Security Question:
Answer:
Notes:

Website:
URL:
Username:
Password:
Email:

Security Question: ______________________________

Answer: ______________________________

Notes: ______________________________

W

Website:

URL:

Username:

Password:

Email:

Security Question:

Answer:

Notes:

Website:

URL:

Username:

Password:

Email:

Security Question:

Answer:

Notes:

Website:

URL:

Username:

Password:

Email:

Security Question: ______________________________

Answer: ______________________________

Notes: ______________________________

X

X

Website:

URL:

Username:

Password:

Email:

Security Question:

Answer:

Notes:

Website:

URL:

Username:

Password:

Email:

Security Question:

Answer:

Notes:

Website:

URL:

Username:

Password:

Email:

Security Question: ________________________________

Answer: ________________________________

Notes: ________________________________

X

Website:

URL:

Username:

Password:

Email:

Security Question:

Answer:

Notes:

Website:

URL:

Username:

Password:

Email:

Security Question:

Answer:

Notes:

Website:

URL:

Username:

Password:

Email:

Security Question: ______________________________

Answer: ______________________________

Notes: ______________________________

X

Website:

URL:

Username:

Password:

Email:

Security Question:

Answer:

Notes:

Website:

URL:

Username:

Password:

Email:

Security Question:

Answer:

Notes:

Website:

URL:

Username:

Password:

Email:

Security Question: ______________________________

Answer: ______________________________

Notes: ______________________________

X

Website: ____________________
URL: ____________________
Username: ____________________
Password: ____________________
Email: ____________________
Security Question: ____________________
Answer: ____________________
Notes: ____________________

Website: ____________________
URL: ____________________
Username: ____________________
Password: ____________________
Email: ____________________
Security Question: ____________________
Answer: ____________________
Notes: ____________________

Website: ____________________
URL: ____________________
Username: ____________________
Password: ____________________
Email: ____________________

Security Question: ____________________

Answer: ____________________

Notes: ____________________

Y

Y

Website:

URL:

Username:

Password:

Email:

Security Question:

Answer:

Notes:

Website:

URL:

Username:

Password:

Email:

Security Question:

Answer:

Notes:

Website:

URL:

Username:

Password:

Email:

Security Question: ___

Answer: ___

Notes: ___

Y

Website:
URL:
Username:
Password:
Email:
Security Question:
Answer:
Notes:

Website:
URL:
Username:
Password:
Email:
Security Question:
Answer:
Notes:

Website:
URL:
Username:
Password:
Email:

Security Question: ______________________________

Answer: ______________________________

Notes: ______________________________

Y

Website:
URL:
Username:
Password:
Email:
Security Question:
Answer:
Notes:

Website:
URL:
Username:
Password:
Email:
Security Question:
Answer:
Notes:

Website:
URL:
Username:
Password:
Email:

Security Question: ______________________________

Answer: ______________________________

Notes: ______________________________

Y

Website:
URL:
Username:
Password:
Email:
Security Question:
Answer:
Notes:

Website:
URL:
Username:
Password:
Email:
Security Question:
Answer:
Notes:

Website:
URL:
Username:
Password:
Email:

Security Question: ______________________________

Answer: ______________________________

Notes: ______________________________

Z

Z

Website:
URL:
Username:
Password:
Email:
Security Question:
Answer:
Notes:

Website:
URL:
Username:
Password:
Email:
Security Question:
Answer:
Notes:

Website:
URL:
Username:
Password:
Email:

Security Question: ______________________________

Answer: ______________________________

Notes: ______________________________

Z

Website:
URL:
Username:
Password:
Email:
Security Question:
Answer:
Notes:

Website:
URL:
Username:
Password:
Email:
Security Question:
Answer:
Notes:

Website:
URL:
Username:
Password:
Email:

Security Question: ______________________________

Answer: ______________________________

Notes: ______________________________

Z

Website: ______

URL: ______

Username: ______

Password: ______

Email: ______

Security Question: ______

Answer: ______

Notes: ______

Website: ______

URL: ______

Username: ______

Password: ______

Email: ______

Security Question: ______

Answer: ______

Notes: ______

Website: ______

URL: ______

Username: ______

Password: ______

Email: ______

Security Question: ______________________________

Answer: ______________________________

Notes: ______________________________

Z

Website:

URL:

Username:

Password:

Email:

Security Question:

Answer:

Notes:

Website:

URL:

Username:

Password:

Email:

Security Question:

Answer:

Notes:

Website:

URL:

Username:

Password:

Email:

Security Question: ______________________________

Answer: ______________________________

Notes: ______________________________

Wi-Fi Passwords

Home Networks

Network Name (SSID): ____________________

Password: ____________________

Router IP Address: ____________________

Admin Username: ____________________

Admin Password: ____________________

Notes: ____________________

Network Name (SSID): ____________________

Password: ____________________

Router IP Address: ____________________

Admin Username: ____________________

Admin Password: ____________________

Notes: ____________________

Network Name (SSID): ____________________

Password: ____________________

Router IP Address: ____________________

Admin Username: ____________________

Admin Password: ____________________

Notes: ____________________

Work Networks

Network Name (SSID): ____________________

Password: ____________________

Router IP Address: ____________________

Admin Username: ____________________

Admin Password: ____________________

Notes: ____________________

Network Name (SSID): ____________________

Password: ____________________

Router IP Address: ____________________

Admin Username: ____________________

Admin Password: ____________________

Notes: ____________________

Network Name (SSID): ____________________

Password: ____________________

Router IP Address: ____________________

Admin Username: ____________________

Admin Password: ____________________

Notes: ____________________

Frequently Visited

Location:

Network Name (SSID):

Password:

Location:

Network Name (SSID):

Password:

Location:

Network Name (SSID):

Password:

Location:

Network Name (SSID):

Password:

Location:

Network Name (SSID):

Password:

Location:

Network Name (SSID):

Password: ______________________

____

Subscription Tracker

Monthly Subscriptions

Use this section to track all services that bill you on a monthly basis. Review it regularly to identify subscriptions you no longer use.

Service: ______________________________

Monthly Cost: ______________ | **Billing Date:** ______________

Username: ______________________________

Password: ______________________________

Cancel URL / Method: ______________________________

Service: ______________________________

Monthly Cost: ______________ | **Billing Date:** ______________

Username: ______________________________

Password: ______________________________

Cancel URL / Method: ______________________________

Service: ______________________________

Monthly Cost: ______________ | **Billing Date:** ______________

Username: ______________________________

Password: ______________________________

Cancel URL / Method: ______________________________

Service: ______________________________

Monthly Cost: ______________________ | **Billing Date:** ______________________

Username: ____

Password: ____

Cancel URL / Method: ____

____

Service: ____

Monthly Cost: ______________________ | **Billing Date:** ______________________

Username: ____

Password: ____

Cancel URL / Method: ____

Service: ______________________________

Monthly Cost: ______________ | **Billing Date:** ______________

Username: ______________________________

Password: ______________________________

Cancel URL / Method: ______________________________

Service: ______________________________

Monthly Cost: ______________ | **Billing Date:** ______________

Username: ______________________________

Password: ______________________________

Cancel URL / Method: ______________________________

Service: ______________________________

Monthly Cost: ______________ | **Billing Date:** ______________

Username: ______________________________

Password: ______________________________

Cancel URL / Method: ______________________________

Service: ______________________________

Monthly Cost: ______________ | **Billing Date:** ______________

Username: ______________________________

Password: ______________________________

Cancel URL / Method: ______________________________

Service: ______________________

Monthly Cost: ______________ | **Billing Date:** ______________

Username: ______________________

Password: ______________________

Cancel URL / Method: ______________________

Service: ______________________

Monthly Cost: ______________ | **Billing Date:** ______________

Username: ______________________

Password: ______________________

Cancel URL / Method: ______________________

Service: ______________________

Monthly Cost: ______________ | **Billing Date:** ______________

Username: ______________________

Password: ______________________

Cancel URL / Method: ______________________

Service: ______________________

Monthly Cost: ______________ | **Billing Date:** ______________

Username: ______________________

Password: ______________________

Cancel URL / Method: ______________________

Service: ______________________

Monthly Cost: ______________ | **Billing Date:** ______________

Username: ______________________

Password: ______________________

Cancel URL / Method: ______________________

Service: ____________________

Monthly Cost: ____________________ | **Billing Date:** ____________________

Username: ____________________

Password: ____________________

Cancel URL / Method: ____________________

Total Monthly Subscriptions Cost: $____________________

Annual Subscriptions

Service:

Annual Cost: | **Renewal Date:**

Username:

Password:

Service:

Annual Cost: | **Renewal Date:**

Username:

Password:

Service:

Annual Cost: | **Renewal Date:**

Username:

Password:

Service:

Annual Cost: | **Renewal Date:**

Username:

Password:

Service:

Annual Cost: ______________________ | **Renewal Date:** ______________________

Username: ____

Password: ____

Service: ____

Annual Cost: ______________________ | **Renewal Date:** ______________________

Username: ____

Password: ____

Service: ____

Annual Cost: ______________________ | **Renewal Date:** ______________________

Username: ____

Password: ____

Service: ____

Annual Cost: ______________________ | **Renewal Date:** ______________________

Username: ____

Password: ____

Service: ____

Annual Cost: ______________________ | **Renewal Date:** ______________________

Username: ____

Password: ____

Service: ________________________________

Annual Cost: ________________ | **Renewal Date:** ________________

Username: ________________________________

Password: ________________________________

Total Annual Subscriptions Cost: $________________

Combined Annual Cost (Monthly x 12 + Annual): $________________

____

Emergency Contacts

Personal Emergency Contacts

Name: ______________________

Relationship: ______________________

Phone: ______________________

Email: ______________________

Name: ______________________

Relationship: ______________________

Phone: ______________________

Email: ______________________

Name: ______________________

Relationship: ______________________

Phone: ______________________

Email: ______________________

Name: ______________________

Relationship: ______________________

Phone: ______________________

Email: ______________________

Name: ______________________

Relationship: ______________________

Phone: ______________________

Email: ______________________________

Financial Institutions

Bank / Institution: ______________________________

Account Type: ______________________________

Phone: ______________________________

Website: ______________________________

Bank / Institution: ______________________________

Account Type: ______________________________

Phone: ______________________________

Website: ______________________________

Bank / Institution: ______________________________

Account Type: ______________________________

Phone: ______________________________

Website: ______________________________

Bank / Institution: ______________________________

Account Type: ______________________________

Phone: ______________________________

Website: ______________________________

Bank / Institution: ______________________________

Account Type: ______________________________

Phone: ______________________________

Website: ________________________________

Insurance

Provider: ______________________________

Policy Number: ______________________________

Phone: ______________________________

Website: ______________________________

Provider: ______________________________

Policy Number: ______________________________

Phone: ______________________________

Website: ______________________________

Provider: ______________________________

Policy Number: ______________________________

Phone: ______________________________

Website: ______________________________

Medical

Doctor / Provider: ____________________

Specialty: ____________________

Phone: ____________________

Address: ____________________

Doctor / Provider: ____________________

Specialty: ____________________

Phone: ____________________

Address: ____________________

Doctor / Provider: ____________________

Specialty: ____________________

Phone: ____________________

Address: ____________________

Security Questions & Answers

Many websites and services use security questions as a backup method for verifying your identity or resetting your password. The problem is that over time, you may forget exactly how you answered a particular question — did you capitalize the city name? Did you use your childhood nickname or your legal name? Did you give a truthful answer or a deliberately false one for extra security?

This section provides a master list where you can record your security question answers in one place. If you use the same set of answers across multiple sites, this reference will ensure you always know the exact spelling and format you used. If you use deliberately incorrect answers for additional security (a recommended practice), this is especially important — you will not be able to guess your way back in without this record.

Question: ____________________

Answer: ____________________

Used On: ____________________

Question: ____________________

Answer: ____________________

Used On: ____________________

Question: ______________________________

Answer: ______________________________

Used On: ______________________________

Question: ______________________________

Answer: ______________________________

Used On: ______________________________

Question: ______________________________

Answer: ______________________________

Used On: ______________________________

Question: ______________________________

Answer: ______________________________

Used On: ______________________________

Question: ______________________________

Answer: ______________________________

Used On: ______________________________

Question: ______________________________

Answer: ______________________________

Used On: ______________________________

Question: ____

Answer: ____

Used On: ____

Question: ____

Answer: ____

Used On: ____

Question: ____

Answer: ____

Used On: ____

Question: ____

Answer: ____

Used On: ____

Question: ____

Answer: ____

Used On: ____

Question: ____

Answer: ____

Used On: ____

Question: ____

Answer: ____

Used On: ____

Notes

Notes

Notes

Notes

Notes

About the Author

For 22 years, Maxwell Stirling awoke each morning not knowing if it would be his last. As a double agent at the heart of Cold War espionage, discovery meant death—not as metaphor, but as literal consequence.

His cover was thorough. Officially, Maxwell was a Soviet diplomat, recruited by the KGB as a young man, stationed across Western European capitals to gather intelligence on NATO activities. He played the role perfectly—so perfectly that he rose to positions of significant trust within Soviet intelligence.

What Moscow didn't know: Maxwell had been working for MI6 since before his supposed KGB recruitment. Every intelligence report he filed was disinformation carefully crafted by British handlers. Every genuine secret he obtained went West. For over two decades, he was a ghost in the machine.

The skills required for this survival are extraordinary and transferable. Reading intentions from microexpressions and body language. Building trust systematically with people trained to trust no one. Managing information asymmetry to maximum advantage. Maintaining multiple identities without psychological fragmentation. Performing flawlessly under pressure where failure meant a bullet.

When the Cold War ended, Maxwell's masters offered retirement with honors. He chose instead to teach what he'd learned. His books translate intelligence tradecraft into business strategy, negotiation technique, and performance psychology. The methods that kept him alive in a world of betrayal now help executives navigate competitive markets, entrepreneurs read investors, and professionals thrive under pressure.

The stakes are rarely as high as Maxwell faced. The skills work regardless.

© 2026 Maxwell Stirling. All rights reserved.

Published by Vuhn

No part of this publication may be reproduced, distributed, or transmitted in any form or by any means without the prior writ-

ten permission of the publisher, except for brief quotations in reviews and certain noncommercial uses permitted by copyright law.

Made in the USA
Monee, IL
05 November 2026

67816265R00187